A WOMAN'S GUIDE TO

TRI ATH LON

THE THINGS MEN WILL NEVER TELL YOU ABOUT THE SPORT

EVA MAUER

Reviews and feedback help improve this book and the author. If you enjoy this book, we would greatly appreciate it if you could take a few moments to share your opinion and post a review on Amazon.

Download the Audio Version of This Book FREE

If you love listening to audiobooks on-the-go or enjoy narration as you read along, I have great news for you. You can download the audio book version of Hygge for FREE just by signing up for a FREE 30-day audible trial!

Click the links below to get started

> > For Audible US < <
http://bit.do/e2KRZ

> > For Audible UK < <
http://bit.do/e2KR5

ISBN: 978-10723-256-1-1

TABLE OF CONTENTS

CHAPTER I:

WHY TRIATHLON

WHAT IS YOUR "WHY"

Right now, you have an idea — you'd like to race a triathlon. At this point, a triathlon might feel like an impossible feat, and you might feel a little overwhelmed even thinking about it. Believe it or not, you can successfully complete a triathlon no matter what level of fitness you are starting from. Give yourself enough time and proper training, and triathlon might very well be the sport for you.

It is important to note that an idea is not going to give you the motivation to get up and go for a bike ride on a Saturday morning when you could very well be sleeping in. You're going to need something a bit more substantial than an idea. Simon Sinek, a renowned expert on motivation and success, suggests that the key to achieving your goals is to be very clear about your "why." This means it is important to be cognizant of the reasons behind the things you are doing. If you want to follow through with your goals, you need to know what is going to motivate you when everything in your body and mind is telling you to stop.

Why is it so important to have a reason to sign up for your first triathlon? In short, training for and completing a triathlon is not easy. Your body will tell you to quit. Your brain will play tricks on you to convince you to give up. Doing difficult things like a triathlon is hugely rewarding, but it is going to require grit, determination, sweat, and probably tears. There will be sacrifices; there will be days when you just don't want to try anymore. Right now, before you start this process, is your chance to be perfectly clear with yourself about why you are doing this.

Humans can do amazing things with enough motivation and a strong "why." Kyle Maynard climbed to the top of Mt. Kilimanjaro. What makes this even more impressive is that Kyle has no arms past the elbow or legs below the knees. How was Kyle able to keep pushing onward toward his summit? He had the ashes of a fallen war hero around his neck. He had promised that hero's wife and child that he would place those ashes on the top of Mt. Kilimanjaro. Despite constant pain and suffering, doing something that felt impossible, Kyle was able to tell a grieving woman that her beloved husband would forever be on top of the world. Kyle took his goal to climb mountains and gave himself a reason, and during many moments of that climb, those ashes were the only thing keeping him going.

When it comes to this wild idea of completing a triathlon, ask yourself, "What is my 'why?'" Figure out the answer now because you will need it. Your "why" needs to be something you are willing to suffer for. Your "why" should not be a trivial matter that won't be important to you in a few weeks. Anyone who tells you that training for a triathlon is easy has clearly never trained for one. Make sure you have a bigger reason to hold onto when the initial excitement of your new idea wears off. If you're unsure of your "why", I'll give you some ideas that have been a source of motivation for other women. Maybe some of them will resonate with you.

HEALTH

There is no need to wait until you are suffering from health concerns to start finding a sport that you love and that will keep your ticker ticking. Triathlon is a great way to strengthen your muscles, including your heart. Endurance sports make your heart and lungs more adept at providing oxygen to your muscles. This is referred to as your VO_2 max. This is the value of how much oxygen is absorbed into your blood from every breath you inhale. As you become more fit, you increase your VO_2 max. In turn, when your body knows how to absorb more oxygen, every action seems a little easier. For example, you won't be winded from making your bed in the morning or walking up stairs. You'll feel more rested because your brain is getting more air. Cardiovascular training improves more than just your heart health — it improves your whole health. You can lower your risk of heart attacks in the future while also improving your quality of life right now.

A KILLER BODY

We live in an era when it is, unfortunately, more important than ever to *look* healthy, not just to *be* healthy. Lean, strong bodies are valued, and looking too thin or too thick becomes a fear for many women. This is unfortunate because true health cannot be measured by appearance. However, it is impossible to hide from reality and pretend that most women don't want to look amazing. Triathlon not only helps you shed any extra weight, but it also builds strength and helps tone your muscles to sculpt your body. Yes, this seems like a selfish "why," but I would be lying to say it is not important for many of us women. I know how important it is to feel good about your body, and the hunt for killer abs is often a great motivation to get out there and train. Just remember to eat well in order to fuel yourself for the training and be patient — a six-pack doesn't appear overnight.

PROVE YOURSELF

How many of you have ever been told you can't do something? When someone doubts you, it spurs you to try even harder to prove them wrong. Completing a triathlon (or many triathlons) is a perfect way to show the world exactly what kind of woman you are. You are a woman who does not back down from a challenge. You are the kind of woman who powers through the suffering of training to make yourself stronger. Use every moment of training, every healthy bite you eat, every mile you log, to demonstrate the strength you've possessed the whole time. To all the doubters you can confidently say, "I've always known I was strong enough, even when you didn't."

Proving your inner strength is amazing motivation and if you don't believe me, try it. Something fantastic happens when you exceed the limited expectations of others. Prove that you can surpass the barriers that others think might stop you.

INSPIRE AND LEAD

Some women are inspired to become mothers. From the first moments of motherhood, they are driven to inspire their children. Mothers want to lead by example. We want our children to see what is possible, and the best way to do that is to *do* what seems impossible. If you are a mother, a sister, an aunt, or in any other role in which the next generation might look up to you, inspiring others is a great source of motivation. Let young girls see you working through obstacles and rising to meet a challenge. Become the person you want them to be. By doing the things you want to be remembered for, you can show them a strong, inspirational woman, tackling the impossible.

WORK OUT YOUR ANGER

There are many things in life that can frustrate you. Most of life feels out of control and chaotic. Your boss will upset you or your spouse will get on your nerves. Maybe you are just feeling mad at yourself and situations beyond your control. It's absolutely fine and natural to be upset with life, as long as you can focus that anger towards doing something productive, something that will improve your overall situation. What better way to work through anger than by training for a triathlon? Stamp out your anger by going all in — not just running or biking but competing in three sports at the same time. The training is intense, but sometimes you'll need intensity to stay focused. Triathlon is not a distraction from your stress. It is not a distraction from the things in life that make you angry. Triathlon is a target for you to throw all your darts of frustration at. It is the focus of your anger. It is the place you can scream and vent, and all of that screaming will give you the emotional fuel to train even harder and push past the limits you thought you had.

Triathlon training is something in your life you can control, and sometimes having that control is the best thing you can do for your mental well-being.

THREE SPORTS ARE BETTER THAN ONE

If you are reading this book, you've already determined that three sports are better than one. Let's face it, you could be training for a marathon and not spending your days smelling like chlorine, or sporting the super-sexy-bike-helmet hairstyle. However, let's talk about why three sports are better (just in case you ever forget or start to question your sanity for wanting to do a triathlon). Consider each sport on its own first.

As with all sports, always make sure you are cleared for training by a medical professional. If you have any concerns about your health at any point during training, speak with your healthcare provider.

RUNNING

Running is one of the fastest and best known ways to shed pounds and lose body fat. Because running is a high-impact sport, your body naturally tries to reduce the impact being placed on your joints. How? By getting rid of as much weight as possible. Long-distance runners have very lean legs for a reason: there is less weight to have to cycle through a run stride. Long-distance runners also tend to have very lean muscles because muscles weigh a lot, and that weight is going to be slammed into knees, hips, and ankles with every footfall. Your body is really smart and it will adapt to your sport, so running long distances will help make you lean and shed excess weight.

In regard to your heart, running will get your heart pumping better than most other activities. Your legs need blood faster to deal with the wear and tear on your muscles and joints, causing your heart to beat faster. During activities with high impact, like running, your heart rate will be around ten beats per minute faster than the beats per minute for less impactful sports. Because of this, running is a great way to build cardiovascular fitness quickly. As you run, your heart becomes stronger and more efficient.

Compared to other endurance sports, such as swimming, running is not technique-based, which means your mind can be a bit freer to wander or shut off as needed. Because conscious thought has a chance to rest, many runners claim that running reduces stress and anxiety. They say it clears their mind, and the repetitive movement helps keep them grounded in the present. What is especially relevant is that running has scientifically proven mental benefits that make runners smarter, more emotionally stable, and happier. There is a new field of research focusing on a protein in the brain called brain-derived neurotrophic factor (BDNF), which is produced in higher quantities after a run. Studies show that BDNF is like Miracle-Gro for brain cells, especially in the areas of our brain association with emotions. This means running can improve our thoughts overall, not just while experiencing a runner's high.

CYCLING

Riding a bike puts much less stress on your joints but requires more power from your muscles than running does; more power means stronger muscles. We have all seen ads from gyms and workout programs promising a bigger butt and flatter stomach. While those programs have their merits, cycling works just as well. Your main source of power for pushing your bike forward, no matter how heavy your bike, is your glute muscles (that's your butt). Unlike running, when you are riding a bike, you're pushing your power down into the pedal rather than forward. You aren't just pushing yourself forward; you're pushing wheels, a frame, handlebars, and all of your other cycling accessories forward. All of that means that your leg and glute muscles need some serious power in order to go faster. This is another example of how our bodies adapt to our sport. When we need more power from our legs, we get stronger, more efficient muscles in our legs and butt.

Additional benefits of cycling are balance and core training. Humans have become experts at standing up without needing to engage many muscles in order to balance. On a bike, the tiny muscles involved with balance are on rapid-fire response, including your abs and core. As you continue riding and your bike handling improves (which it will), your core naturally tightens up to maintain your balance while still moving your legs.

Additionally, because cycling is not as intense of a sport as running, your heart rate will not spike as fast, which gives you time to get in a really solid workout without feeling like you want to faint. This is especially beneficial to beginner athletes who need to be able to maintain a higher heart rate without wearing out too fast.

All the mental benefits of running are present in riding, with the added bonus that your mind develops an ability to become hyper-focused. On a ride, a crash can cause serious pain and injury so your mind will be occupied with focusing on the road or trail in front of you in order to prevent that. This is beneficial because many of us do not have enough opportunities in our indoor, sedentary lives to practice hyperfocus.

SWIMMING

You might not sweat as much during a swim and you might not shed the pounds, but swimming is by far the best workout to train your mind and body without overwhelming stress on your joints and muscles.

Swimming is an endurance sport that works the whole body, especially the upper body, so be prepared to have sculpted shoulders and triceps. Your back will be ripped with muscles in no time from the force needed to push against the resistance of water. You can also expect to learn how to breathe effectively to provide power and avoid inhaling water — a skill that will help you in many other sports.

Because swimming is highly technical, your mind is always active and focusing on your proprioception — the awareness of where your body is in relation to its surroundings. Swimming does not allow your mind to wander and keeps you in the present. This improves your self-awareness and knowledge of what pieces of your body are doing at any given time.

THREE SPORTS TOGETHER

With all the benefits of running, cycling, and swimming on their own, it's easy to see why combining the three is even more beneficial. You get the lean muscle tone from running without losing the strength you gain from cycling. You can lose yourself in thought and be free from negativity while running but still train your mind to focus and concentrate while cycling and swimming. When combined, these three sports train you to become aware of your surroundings as well as of your own person. You learn how to breathe smoothly and evenly with a steady heart rate from swimming, while still getting the cardio benefits of a highly elevated heart rate from running. You can have sculpted shoulders, butt, and legs from the use of multiple muscle groups.

Training for any endurance sport has benefits, but triathletes get all the benefits of three sports, plus training for three different sports is never boring. When you are bored with running every day, you can hop on your bike and switch it up. If you just can't stomach another day in the pool, take a jog around the block a few times instead.

At this stage, you are also enthusiastic about triathlon. Congratulations! You are on the path to learning exciting skills, gaining fantastic fitness, joining a support community, and having unparalleled adventures.

CHAPTER 2:

TRAINING BASICS

You might be under the assumption that training for a triathlon only involves swimming, biking, and running, but that's only half the work. Yes, you will need to get better in each discipline, and you will spend your time practicing these three activities, but training is much more involved than just putting in the sweat and physical effort.

TIME MANAGEMENT

The first thing you will realize as soon as you glance at a triathlon training plan is the time commitment. It's not a large time commitment. You can easily train for a triathlon in the same time you may devote to working out now — a minimum of six hours a week. Can you devote the time to training? Probably. Often you can multitask and combine some quality TV time with time on a stationary bike or listen to an audiobook while you run.

The actual number of hours is not as intimidating as making the timing work. Swim training must be done when the lap lanes at your pool are open or when you can access some open water. Bike training (if done on a road) should be when there is little traffic and when it is light outside for safety reasons. Running is the easiest to fit in, but you'll still need to account for added time to shower and change out of your sweaty running clothes.

The best way to plan for the time restrictions of triathlon training is to start with the least flexible activity — swimming. When will you be able to get in your laps or your open water swims? (Yes, swimming in open water is important.) Find two to three times during the week to focus on your swimming, and work those into your schedule first. Next, work in times when you will be able to hop on a bike and push your pedals. Lastly, fit in your running workouts around the other disciplines, as it is much easier to find a time and a place for a run.

Remember that for every activity there is an appropriate level of hygiene to deal with afterward. This should also be planned into your time management system. After a swim, always rinse off.

Your suit, skin, and especially your hair will thank you. If you have time a full shower is nice, but as long as you are able to at least rinse the chlorine or saline from your body, that's often enough until you can shower later. No matter what type of swim cap you wear, you cannot maintain a perfect style during a swim, so schedule time to reapply makeup and do your hair as needed. Plan accordingly! Planning for hygiene is part of training. Don't cut your workouts short because you forgot to plan for a shower.

When riding a bike, you will probably be wearing a cycling kit because triathletes wear a lot of spandex. In the crotch of your cycling shorts there is a nice, comfy cushion/pad called a chamois (pronounced shammy). If you are wearing strictly triathlon shorts, the chamois isn't super comfy but is still soft. Whatever cycling shorts you are wearing, they are designed to NOT be worn with underwear, which means you're going to be sweating directly into your shorts. After your ride, plan time to change out of your sweaty clothes. Trust me — you want to have a few minutes to save yourself from the chafing that happens from sitting on a wet chamois for too long. After a run or ride, your clothes will be extra sweaty and if you don't give yourself a few minutes to change clothes, those wet shirts and shorts can leave your body chilled as you cool down.

Plan time to eat after you train. There is nothing worse than finishing up a really tough run and not having time to replenish those lost calories. You will understand quickly that food is all you can think about sometimes when you're burning through a lot of energy. Pack a healthy snack, and make sure you have time to enjoy it.

BASIC GEAR

Each triathlon sport has its own special toolbox of gear. Some of these are obvious, like a swimsuit, but not everything is as intuitive. There are many options out there, and it's nice to just know what you need without having to make hard decisions.

Use this simple guide to make sure you have the required gear to get started. Additional gear can always be added over time, but you can effectively complete your first triathlon with just these basics.

SWIMMING

Suit — You'll want a sport swimsuit that stays in place, is comfortable, and keeps you covered. You don't want to lose time adjusting a poor-fitting suit.

Goggles — Try them on before buying. Goggles need to fit snugly without leaking or pinching.

Swim cap — Invest in a good latex or silicone cap. It's nicer on your hair and smoother in the water.

Pool pass — Since you'll need time in the pool to train, check out the pool options nearby before you commit to training.

Optional: **Wetsuit** — these can be rented and may not be required for all races. This depends on the location of your race.

BIKING

Bike — Go to a professional bike store to be properly sized before you go bike shopping. Buy a bike that is appropriate for the type of triathlon you are doing. Do not buy a mountain bike if you are doing a road triathlon. When buying your first bike, I highly recommend speaking with someone who is experienced with triathlons. For your first race you will not need a time trial bike, but you will need something that will be comfortable for long-distance rides. Look up some bike shops close by, and explain that you are training for your first triathlon.

Chain lube and degreaser — Bikes require maintenance. Take care of your bike by cleaning the grease off and then lubing the chain to keep your tires spinning with ease.

Extra tubes and tire levers — Chances are high that you will have a flat tire at some point during your training. Learn to change tires before hitting the road. You may need help at first but having the proper tools will always make the process easier.

Water bottles and bottle holders — Some bikes come with bottle holders;Use them. Staying hydrated is always important.

Cycling shorts — Cycling shorts are designed to be comfortable to ride in. Specially created triathlon shorts are going to be much more comfortable than regular shorts, as they are designed without any seams or pockets to irritate your skin. After a few long rides without cycling shorts, you'll appreciate the difference. Again, cycling shorts are intended to be worn without underwear.

A bike mechanic — While this technically isn't gear, your bike is a machine that needs to be serviced, just like your car. Find a good bike mechanic and stick with them.

HELMET — I'm putting this in capital letters because you should never ride your bike without a helmet. Some races won't even let you touch your bike without a helmet.

RUNNING

Shoes — The cause for sore feet, knees, hips, and back is almost always bad footwear. Buy a pair of running shoes that fit well and are appropriate for your training conditions.

Sports bra — Look for a sports bra that will minimize bouncing but does not rub on your skin. Avoid cotton bras that will soak up water and sweat and cause irritation.

Running shorts — Shorts are designed to prevent chafing and keep you dry. Shorts with a built-in pocket are great for storing your keys or other small necessities.

Water bottle — There are options for how to bring water onto your runs. Hydration packs can be worn on your back, around your hips, or in a hand strap. During the race, there are aid stations which provide hydration, but for training you will need to bring your own.

Optional: Race belt — You will put your race number onto a belt for the run portion of the triathlon. Sometimes you can borrow these or pin the number to any cloth belt that is easy to snap on.

GENERAL

Phone app — It's very helpful to be able to track your speed, distance, and location during your bikes and runs. A few options are Track my Ride, Track my Run, or Strava. Find one that works for you. Most are free.

Optional: **Phone holder** — If your phone doesn't fit in your pocket or you don't want to hold it, invest in a secure way to store your phone on your body during your workouts.

Nutrition — I'll go over this more in following chapters, but you will need food that gives you energy for training and can replace electrolytes lost from sweat.

There are many more things you might see triathletes wearing or using to train; however, this is a list of the bare basics to get you started. Even on a modest budget, these items should get any intrepid trainer ready for race day.

WOMEN-SPECIFIC CONCERNS

There are a few special concerns for women while training for a triathlon. No need to worry — just know that female athletes are strong and capable, no matter what.

Hormones and hormonal changes are a real thing, and they can affect your training. There will be days when you feel stronger than ever, like nothing can stop you. There will also be days when you cannot seem to get into a rhythm, and training feels pointless. Be aware that this is normal for women, and our training fluctuates a lot based on our menstrual cycles. Do what you can when you can, and forgive yourself for the less-than-perfect days. Plus, don't be ashamed to express emotions during your training. There isn't an athlete alive who hasn't cried, become frustrated, or cussed up a storm during training or on a particularly bad day.

Speaking of cycles, how can you train during your period? I recommend using a menstrual cup to avoid issues like leaking and chafing. A cup can be left in for long periods of time without fear of toxic shock syndrome, and you don't have to carry a spare with you. If you prefer using tampons, be sure to change them before training to prevent leaking. Over-the-counter medications such as ibuprofen can ease the pain from cramps without affecting performance.

The thing to remember when your body seems to reject training is that you are doing this triathlon for fun. Ease up on training for a day or two, and go for an easy run or bike ride. If swimming makes you uncomfortable during those days, don't go. This is not supposed to be so serious that you can't still live your life how you need to.

It might seem embarrassing, but sometimes the impact of running can cause an athlete to lose control of bodily functions. During a training run, feel free to stop at restrooms as often as needed. For training, you might also consider wearing a pad or panty liner. Also consider bringing a small bit of toilet paper in a plastic baggie for emergencies. During a race, triathlon kits are very good at masking any urine leaks. Also know that it has happened to other women. It may seem gross, but women athletes understand completely.

What about hair? To protect your hair from the rigors of sweat and chlorine, women in the sport recommend braids and conditioner. Put conditioner in your hair before you put it into your swim cap, and wear braids as often as possible when training to keep your hair from breaking from the use of bands and hair ties.

Skin care during training can be a little different than what you are currently practicing. Moisturize your skin after a swim. Chlorine tends to dry out your skin and cause irritation. Always wash off chlorine and then apply moisturizer. Do *not* moisturize before a run or a bike ride. You want to have your pores open for your sweat to clean out any toxins. Moisturizers can block your pores and cause you to sweat more as your body tries to clean them out. Rinse your face after a particularly sweaty workout. The salt from your sweat can cause dry skin, especially on sensitive facial skin. Always use proper sunscreen when training outdoors. Look for sunscreens that are sweat resistant and will not run into your eyes.

FUN AND SUFFERING

The last thing to note before you start is the importance of training your mind to have fun but also to deal with suffering. You are most likely not a professional athlete. You do not need to dedicate your life to this sport. You are having a new experience, and no matter why you are choosing to try a triathlon, you want to enjoy the entire training process.

I'm not saying you should be having fun on every run. You probably won't like swimming by lap number twenty, and you will be cursing to yourself about your aching butt halfway through your bike ride. Not every moment of training is going to be fun, but the overall effect should be enjoyable. Triathlon is in your life to improve it, so have fun with it.

Similarly, completing a triathlon is probably one of the hardest things you will ever do. You are going to suffer. You will have blisters, chafing, and sunburns. Your muscles will ache, and your joints will occasionally be stiff. Your mind will scream at you to stop and will demand more rest. This is a great way to find comfort in being uncomfortable. Practice suffering. During the race, you are going to be in pain. You are going to wonder why you are doing this, but if you have learned how to cope with suffering and you have let yourself enjoy the process, nothing will stop you from finishing your first triathlon.

It's time to dive in, get things rolling, and put your best foot forward. Let's get started.

CHAPTER 3:

YOUR FIRST TRI

FINDING A RACE

You've got the gear, and you're ready to get going with this new adventure. You're going to need a specific race to claim as your first triathlon.

There are a number of different factors that will influence which race you should choose.

LOCATION

Racing is a great excuse to travel, but because triathlon requires you to transport a bike, sometimes it is better to start locally. A great way to find races is to look on sites like Trifind. com or to do a Google search for "triathlons near [your city]." One thing to remember when looking for races online is to check the year of the race posting. Sometimes calendars are carried over from previous years, so make sure you're looking at current or future races.

If you do want to travel to a race, arrive a few days early. Familiarize yourself with the course, and become acclimated to the climate/ elevation. Traveling can be taxing on the body, so it is important to give yourself a few days to rest before your race.

FRIENDS

Yes, races are always more fun when you are doing them with a friend. Do you have friends who are signing up for the same race as you? What event are they choosing? If you are planning to race alone, what is a race that your friends and family will be able to attend to support you?

DISTANCE

For your first triathlon, you might not want to sign up for a full Ironman-distance race. Generally, a great starting distance is a sprint triathlon or an Olympic-distance tri. A sprint distance includes a roughly 400–500 meter swim, a 20 km bike ride and a 5 km run. Olympic-distance tris are composed of a 750-1500 meter swim, a 40 km ride, and a 10 km run. This is essentially twice the distance of a sprint tri.

If you are new to racing, start out with a sprint tri and work up from there. Remember you are there to have fun, not to overwhelm yourself during training and get burnt-out.

STYLE

Right now, there are two types of triathlons: on-road (often just referred to as road) and off-road (sometimes called Xterra). Road triathlons often feature an open-water swim, although sometimes the swim portion is held in a pool. The bike ride is along a paved road, and the run is usually also along pavement. An off-road triathlon includes an open-water swim with a mountain-bike ride and a trail run.

FINDING A TRAINING PLAN

Now that you have selected your triathlon, the next step is to find or create a training plan that works for you. You need to be aware of how many weeks you have until race day and select a plan that will keep you training with the best results right up until you are ready to jump into the water.

Training plans can be basic or complicated, and often the prices of the plan correspond to the complexity. Basic training plans are really all you need at this stage and there are hundreds of them online, many of which are free.

Many plans can be printed and taped to your refrigerator for easy reference. Remember to tailor the training plan to fit into your schedule. This is where your time management practice comes in. You might have to change a few things around, but for a beginner, this shouldn't be too much of a problem. If it is in your budget, you can also hire a coach to customize a plan for you. You can also join a team, but we will talk more about that later.

Remember that your goal for this first race is not to win, it is to finish. Stick to the training plan you select, but if you struggle here and there, don't stress. Have fun and enjoy the process of getting stronger, faster, and fitter. Winning races can come later. Right now, you should be focused on all the other benefits you are getting from training for triathlon.

Whatever you do, do not overtrain. Because triathlon includes three sports, it is easy to become consumed by training and overwhelm yourself. If you are burnt-out, triathlon will no longer be fun, and you could be causing physical problems which can lead to injury. Take rest days when they are called for in your training plan, and listen to your body. No overtraining, deal?

CHAPTER 4:

KEEPING TRACK OF YOUR TRAINING

There are two ways to look at your triathlon training: planning or pantsing (pantsing means going by the seat of your pants). The problem with training without a plan in place is that there is no way to really track your progress and be aware of your improvements. Some people like the spontaneity, but I personally never recommend trying to enter your first triathlon without a plan of action, as well as a plan B.

The benefit of using a plan for training is that it makes tracking your progress exceptionally easy. With automated apps, your training data is often tracked for you. If you are not using an app, you can track your progress by handwriting comments and statistics about your workouts on the training plan itself or in a journal.

Why do you need to track your training? Confidence. As you get into this sport and meet other athletes or follow other women on Strava, Facebook, or Instagram, you'll instinctively want to compare yourself to them. That's natural, but it can sometimes be demoralizing. You are a beginner, and there are going to be people who are faster than you. There will be women who can fly through the run portion of the tri before you have even tied your shoes. It's easy to get sucked into a cyclone of negativity and self-doubt. Fight back against that by being aware of how far you've come since you started.

I have a log of my first run, and it helps me remember how much I've improved. On my first run, I ran at a twelve-and-a-half-minute-mile pace for three minutes. Then I walked for two minutes. I repeated this eight times. When I got home, I collapsed in a useless pile on the floor. I was completely spent, and I hadn't even covered three miles.

I spend a lot of time following professional athletes and training with women who fly by me like I've got glue on my feet. It's easy to get sucked into comparison games, but when I do, I go back and look at the log of my early runs. I look at my progress. I am honestly proud of my accomplishments, and I am the only triathlete I should be comparing myself to.

I know this is especially difficult for women because we have such a tendency to be social. A side effect of getting out and spending time with other women is a natural drive to compare ourselves to them. Track your workouts, and keep a log of what you've accomplished as a reminder that the woman you are comparing yourself to is the woman you were before — not the women you are having cocktails or coffee with.

Another excellent reason for tracking your workouts is to become aware of your strengths and weaknesses.

If you are noticing that you are not making much improvement in your running pace, you can adjust training to include an extra little run each week. Triathlon training is always a balancing act to improve your weak discipline while maintaining the strengths you've gained in the other disciplines. For your first triathlon this might not be as relevant, but it will be very important in future races since you will know where you will struggle and where you will excel.

The easiest way to keep a training log is through an app. I like Training Peaks, which allows me to add comments to all of my workouts and can be integrated with a lot of GPS devices. If you don't have a lot of gadgets, Strava or MapMyRun/Ride are good options as well. Alternatively, you can print your training plan out and leave space each day to fill in the details of each workout.

There are four things you'll want to track: pace, distance, perceived exertion (or heart rate if you have a heart rate monitor), and nutrition.

PACE

This is how fast you are going. For the swim, you will more than likely have to track your own pace. Swim pace is referenced for every 100 yards. Most likely you will be swimming in a 25-yard pool. A length is one length of the pool from one wall to the opposite wall, or 25 yards. A lap is the distance measured by swimming to the opposite wall and back, or 50 yards. Pace, therefore, is calculated based on how long it takes for you to swim two laps.

Most pools have a clock near the start of the lap lanes. Push off the wall when the second hand is at zero. Swim one lap and note how long it takes you. For your pace, multiply that number by two (for two laps, or 100 yards).

Example: You swim one lap in 1 minute 10 seconds. Your pace is 2:20 / 100 yards. If you swim one lap in 40 seconds, your pace is 1:20 / 100 yards.

You don't need to track your pace for every lap you swim, but be sure to use it as a reference for your log.

Cycling pacing is done by speed just like in a car: miles per hour or kilometers per hour. Apps such as Strava can track your speed over the duration of your bike ride.

A running pace is referred to as the time it takes for you to run one mile (or kilometer, depending on your standard of measurement). If you have a ten-minute pace, that means you can run one mile in ten minutes. When I say I started running at a 12:30 pace, it means I would run a mile at that speed in twelve-and-a-half minutes. An easy walking pace is generally around sixteen-to-twenty-minute miles. An elite-level sprinter would run at a 4:30 mile. You'll fall somewhere in the middle. Phone apps can help you track this as well.

DISTANCE

Depending on the distance you plan to race, you might need to start adding longer workouts into your training to ensure that you will be fit enough to finish your tri. In your training log, you will need to track how far you swim, bike, and run to know the distance you can cover.

Swimming — As mentioned before, you will probably be swimming in a 25-yard pool. 33 laps will be a mile swim for you. If you are doing a sprint distance tri, you will probably be swimming the equivalent of 15 laps for your race. Work up to the distance you need to accomplish in your triathlon.

Biking and running can be tracked with an app, but it's nice to know a few routes that are approximately the right distance. Some apps have recommended routes, and feel free to search on Google for ideas. If you keep track of places you ride and run, you can start finding your own routes. Track how far you ride and run each week to make sure that the distance of your tri is within shooting range.

PERCEIVED EXERTION (HEART RATE)

If you have a heart rate monitor, great. If not, you can track your rate of perceived exertion (RPE) for each workout. RPE is tracked on a scale of 1–10. One is essentially no exertion, and ten is the hardest effort you could possibly put forth. If RPE was converted to a heart rate, generally one equals your resting heart rate, and ten is your maximum heart rate. Combine RPE or heart rate with your pace, and you will know how difficult it is for you to hold that pace for the duration of a race.

Often coaches and trainers will refer to different training zones. They are referring to your heart rate and your perceived exertion. The following zones are not accurate for everyone but act as a rough guide:

- ✔ **Zone 1:** Recovery — RPE 1–3 — Most individuals could be in the zone for multiple hours without feeling fatigued.
- ✔ **Zone 2:** Endurance — RPE 2–4 — This is equal to a brisk walk — a triathlete would have no problem here for a long endurance workout.
- ✔ **Zone 3:** Tempo — RPE — 4–6 — You could probably keep this up for an hour if you had to, but you will be sweating a lot and it would hurt.

- ✔ **Zone 4:** Threshold — RPE — 6-8 — This is the maximum of what you could do for thirty minutes to an hour. This is a good, solid effort.
- ✔ **Zone 5:** Anaerobic — RPE — 9 — You would struggle to hold this for a few minutes, and your body must adjust to the higher energy demands.
- ✔ **Zone 5+:** Sprint — RPE — 9-10 — This is an all-out effort with everything you've got for a short amount of time. You would not be able to maintain this effort for long.

Some apps allow you to track your zones and determine the amount of time you spent in each. Keep track of your perceived exertion for the main part of each workout and also the perceived exertion for the warmup and cooldown. This will give you ideas about how long your body takes to warm up and to recover.

NUTRITION

When I refer to tracking your nutrition, I don't mean you should keep track of everything you eat. If you choose to do that, it's fine, but that is not what I am referring to for your training log. Triathlons are intense and require you to have proper fuel and electrolytes. Triathlons can also be extremely hard on your stomach if you are fueling it with something your body does not appreciate. Everyone is different. There is no rule about what to eat or not to eat, which is why it is up to you to keep track of what works and what doesn't work.

If eating a spoonful of peanut butter before a workout gives you terrible side cramps, track that so you don't do it again — I speak from experience. Likewise, if running after a cup of coffee in the morning makes your stomach do flips, keep a log of that so you can time your morning coffee better.

If a banana tastes too sweet after two hours on a bike, what other food could you try? Maybe a snack of salty rice is the perfect pre-workout fuel. Part of training is learning what works for you and what doesn't. Get to know your body and what foods you are craving and then write that down so you are more aware as you head towards race day.

Training is a perfect time to keep track of your activities and experiences so that on race day you can look back at your training and feel confident in what you have learned and accomplished. You have put in the work, and you have proof that you can complete this triathlon. You can make some educated guesses about how long it will take and where you will struggle the most. This is the knowledge you need to push through the mental barriers of getting out and competing.

CHAPTER 5:

REST AND RECOVERY

For every difficult workout you put in, you need to let your body heal. When you are just starting out, the best thing you can do for yourself is to make sure you give your body and your mind time to recover from the work it is doing. Rest and recovery are just as important as going for a swim, a bike ride, and a run.

What happens in your body during a hard workout? First, your heart is beating much harder and faster than normal. Your muscles are contracting and sometimes tearing due to the extra stress from perpetual motion. Your joints are constantly grinding against each other as you go through the motions needed for each sport. Your lungs are pulling in a ton of air and working to sift out the beneficial oxygen and eliminate the carbon dioxide at an accelerated rate. The cells of your body are working to convert calories into energy and disperse that energy throughout your body. Blood vessels are expanding to allow the increased amount of blood flow to pass through, and your pores are converting extra water in your body to sweat to keep you cool.

Without even considering yet what happens in your brain, it's clear that your body is doing a ton of work and it deserves a little bit of rest.

What do recovery and rest look like for a beginner triathlete? There are a few major components of recovery you should never forget.

SLEEP

By now you have heard that the average adult needs seven to eight hours of sleep. The average athlete needs as much sleep as she can get. I am all for waking up early to go for a run if that is the time you have available, but if you are shorting yourself on a full night's sleep in order to do that — don't. Go for a shorter run and get thirty extra minutes of sleep if you have to.

Sleep is the time when your body can fully regrow damaged tissue like torn muscles or worn-down joints. In sleep, your heart can beat slowly and steadily while adapting to the demands of training. It is sleep that will allow your mind to cleanse itself of stress with a fresh dose of cortisol, so you can be fresh and happy the following day. Sleep is your best friend, and if you are trying to push yourself too hard without enough sleep for more than a few days, the workouts you put in will not be worth it. Any benefit you gain from a workout is lost when you do not sleep enough.

In addition to a full night's sleep, feel free to take power naps when needed as well. A power nap only needs to be ten to fifteen minutes but can help you become alert and ready to focus on the rest of your day. Power naps are especially helpful after a swim because swimming is so mentally exhausting that oftentimes your brain will feel fatigued. During a power nap, you might not even feel like you've been asleep. That's fine. Just set a timer for fifteen minutes, close your eyes, and eliminate any distractions. Your brain and body will thank you.

REST DAYS

Triathletes have a pretty intense training schedule because we have three sports to practice, not just one. Because of this, we often feel guilty or become anxious whenever we take a rest day. Rest days are still a needed part of training. Your body can reset a bit every night, but after about a week of training, you will need to have a massive recovery. This is especially true for new athletes, like you. Your body has not adapted to the increased stress. Without rest days, you will be prone to more muscle and bone injuries. The more your body adjusts to the new workouts, the longer you can go without a full rest day, but keep in mind that even professional athletes take full days to completely relax.

If you are just feeling too anxious on your rest days and you have to get a workout in, try some of these ideas:

✔ At the pool, rather than swimming laps, practice floating and rotating in the water. Sit in the hot tub to loosen tight muscles. Play in the pool with your kids to become comfortable moving in different ways in the water.

✔ On the bike, ride to a coffee shop or just around your neighborhood. Practice bike handling skills in front of your house. Run some errands on your bike rather than taking the car.

✔ Rather than running, go for a walk or a hike. Stretch your feet, ankles, and calves. Dance and get your body moving without the impact of running.

✔ Spend some time working on the important triathlon training that is often overlooked, like balance and small muscle training. Yoga is a great way to improve balance and stretch your muscles. Small muscle training for your rotator cuffs in your shoulders or the muscles in the bottom of your feet is great rest-day training — as long as you don't get your heart rate up too much.

STRETCHING

Like every athlete in every activity, you should be stretching before and after each workout already. Additionally, try to make stretching part of your rest and recovery process. Many of us forget to stretch after a workout, but it needs to be done.

As your muscles are developed, they tend to form knots or kinks. Think of this like scar tissue that sticks out from your skin. Your muscles need to be stretched and smoothed out to help prevent these knots from forming, as well as to get rid of the knots that already exist. If you have a foam roller, make sure you are rolling out the muscles in your legs and glutes (your butt). Stretch your shoulders and back as well, to save your shoulders in the water. Knots in your muscles are more than just uncomfortable; they decrease how much power you can get from that muscle. A muscle is designed to expand and contract, but every little glitch in the smooth muscle fibers makes it more difficult for that muscle to function. Sometimes stretching or foam rolling hurts, but it's a good kind of hurt. Your muscles are secretly thanking you for releasing them.

When you are stretching, remember to breathe. Muscles need oxygen, especially when those knots are releasing. Whatever you do, don't hold your breath when you stretch. That precious oxygen will help your muscles perform later.

MASSAGE, BATHS, HEAT, AND ICE

Sometimes recovery isn't just about sleep and less movement. There are a few great tools you can use to help your body recover from the beating it takes during training.

Schedule a massage to work out the tough knots that aren't released from just stretching. Look for a deep tissue massage, and don't be afraid of a little pressure. Some people report feeling tired and lethargic after a deep tissue massage, so schedule one on a rest day to be safe.

Take an Epsom salt bath. You can buy Epsom salt at any grocery store or pharmacy. Epsom salt is the shelf name of magnesium sulfate, and it has been known to decrease inflammation and promote healing. An added benefit is that many Epsom salts are now scented with essential oils that have their own healing properties, like ginger to remove toxins, or lavender to ease stress. Add approximately two cups of salts to a warm bath of water and soak for at least twenty minutes. Not only does it feel amazing, but it's a great gift to aching muscles.

Cuddling with a heat pack when your muscles are tight is another great treat for the body. Heat loosens your muscles and eases some of the tension that forms during intense training. If you don't have a heat pack, fill a cloth bag with raw rice and heat it in the microwave for a few minutes. The rice retains the heat for a long time so you can enjoy the warmth.

Ice any potential injuries. Extreme cold from an ice pack is great for sharp pains or injuries. If you feel like you are pushing too hard, have swelling, or are just worried about an ache that seems like it might be a precursor to an injury, apply cold. You can freeze the same pack you made with rice, or you can use ice by itself. Avoid leaving ice directly on your skin for too long. You can also submerge the afflicted area into an ice bath, which is a mixture of equal parts ice and water.

HYDRATE

Part of recovery is making sure you get enough fluids. It is important to drink while you are training, but it is equally important to stay hydrated during the rest of the day as well. Some great ways to stay hydrated are drinking warm tea, eating watery fruits and veggies like watermelon or cucumber, flavoring your water with water enhancers like Mio, snacking on frozen berries, freezing portions of your energy drink to make energy popsicles, or adding extra water to a smoothie snack.

Dehydration will affect your training and can suppress your immune system, so taking in enough water is a huge part of training. If you ever start to feel dizzy during your training or during your recovery, first make sure you are cleared to train from a licensed professional, then check to make sure you are well hydrated and have enough electrolytes in your system. Low blood pressure or dizziness is a clear indication you are not getting enough electrolytes or are dehydrated. Electrolytes are the components of the salts that we lose in sweat. We need electrolytes to function and to think clearly. There are some great products to restore your electrolytes, but most sports drinks will do the trick. For most beginner athletes, one bottle of sports drink for every two to three hours will do, but as always, do what works for you.

During a race, a rule of thumb is to drink one water bottle for every hour of work. When you are not training, you can test your hydration levels with a simple test: drink a large glass of water and time how long before you feel the urge to urinate. If it takes more than an hour, you should probably have some more water in your system.

CHAPTER 6:

COACHING AND TEAMS

Often one of the first things I am asked about getting into triathlon is, "Do I need a coach?" The short answer is no; you can effectively train to complete a triathlon on your own. As a beginner, it is not required to follow a specific plan or have ongoing feedback from an expert.

However, an equally important question I will pose to you is, "Do you want and can you afford a coach?" Having a coach does not always need to be a huge expense. Often coaches work with small groups and teams and will give the same workouts to everyone on the team. This is especially rewarding for beginners because triathlon instantly becomes a community sport.

Choosing to work with a coach or a team is a personal decision. Before you choose, here are some of the drawbacks and benefits of having a coach or joining a team.

First, the drawbacks. Coaching and becoming part of a team are an investment; it costs money and time. Often the team will have group workouts, which may require you to commute and take more of your time. In addition to paying for the coaching services, teams sometimes suggest you purchase a kit, or triathlon outfit you will wear during training and racing to represent the team during your race. You don't need a full kit to race successfully, but sometimes it is expected if you join a team.

When you are training with a coach, you will often adapt to their training style. You might have ideas about what you can or cannot do, and unless you have done a lot of research to find a great coach that fits your style, your coach might have different thoughts. Coaches come in many shapes, styles, and mindsets. It takes a lot of research to find one that works perfectly for you. Even professional athletes have to change coaches sometimes because they realize that a coach does not share the same training philosophy. Know that finding a good coach that matches your mindset is going to take time and might result in some frustration. In contrast, following a plan without a coach lets you adapt without feeling like you need to explain yourself.

Now, onto the benefits of hiring a coach or joining a team. The biggest and overall best thing about having a team is being part of a community. Pick up your official team T-shirt and you will immediately feel accepted, no questions asked. Loneliness is a problem that many women struggle with, and being accepted as part of a group is fulfilling on such a deep, profound level. Not every group is the same, but there is something special about fitness groups that creates a genuine bond almost instantly. Perhaps it's the shared suffering.

Triathlon teams and working with a coach give us a connection with others who understand our struggles. Something about this feeling of shared suffering makes forming relationships easy. By being part of a tri team, you know you have something in common with everyone in the group. Every member is training or working towards a similar goal. This is not a trivial matter, and it can create a feeling of cohesiveness that is not often found in work or even families. The feeling of being part of a triathlon community is often worth the price of membership. Lucky for you, there are also free groups of triathletes who are eager to welcome new members. They might not offer all the other benefits such as coaching or training plans, but the sense of community is there.

Teams generally range in expertise and are a great way to learn from someone who has more experience than you. Coaches are often the primary source for knowledge, so if you choose to hire a coach, use this person as a guide and a resource for all your questions. Knowledge is your best tool for fighting fear and nervousness. Even if you think you are asking silly questions, your coach or someone on your team will know the answer, and that can make this whole experience so much more enjoyable.

Training alone can often be difficult, and it becomes easy to skip workouts when there is no one holding you accountable. We have all been in that position. Staying in bed seems like a much better option compared to having to jump in freezing-cold water and wear yourself out with laps in the pool before 7:00 a.m. If you have teammates who are dealing with the same battle of waking up to train, you have instant accountability. If they can do it, so can you.

You may also find that you enjoy working out with other people, and teammates make great workout partners because they are often in a similar (or identical) training program. Having someone to train with makes long runs or rides much easier because you can talk about your concerns, struggles, and triumphs along the way. It's amazing how effective conversation is at passing the time. Plus, a good workout partner will push you to work harder and dig deeper than you thought you could. Just the presence of another person triggers our minds to put out more effort towards our goals. Some subconscious part of our minds wants to impress those around us and so we are less likely to give up if someone we know can see us.

There are benefits to having a coach beyond the team component. Have you ever had a big plan or a huge project and just never completed it? One of the biggest reasons people don't reach their goals is that they lack the knowledge of how to break the goal down into manageable steps. A coach is going to break down your training into bite-sized pieces that you can swallow rather than focusing on the end result. On top of that, a coach will tell you exactly what needs to be done and when. A coach will then go over your strengths and weaknesses with you to make sure you are getting the most effective training.

Training for a triathlon becomes substantially easier when you have a group behind you supporting you towards your goal. Plus, with a group, you can support others, which has been shown to improve motivation. When you are struggling with doubts or negative thoughts, offer support to someone else in your group. Positivity runs two ways: you receive inspiration and support from others around you, but you can also give it.

Even without a dedicated team, I highly suggest finding some groups of triathletes to spend time with. Train with your peers because there is so much to be gained when you don't go into this alone. You might not need a coach, but you do need someone by your side. If you don't have anyone yet, start by looking at your local running store and asking about recreational running groups. Most are free, and because running is the most popular of the three disciplines of triathlon, you will probably find many people who are willing to run with you at whatever pace you can maintain.

Swimming is a little bit of a different beast when it comes to coaching. Swimming is very technical, and unless you have a background in swimming, there is a high likelihood you have an inefficient stroke.

It is not required to have a dedicated swim coach, but learning from a knowledgeable swimmer is priceless. At a minimum, you'll want to get someone to come to a pool with you and review your swim stroke from the front and the side. It's difficult to fix stroke problems without seeing them to begin with.

If you are going to hire a coach, you can make the most improvements with a swim coach. A swim coach can help you build a stroke that is efficient and fast. Swim coaches do not have to be local either. With new technology, you can film your swims and a virtual coach can help you perfect your stroke online.

If hiring a swim coach is not in the budget for you, look into a masters club at your local pool. Often the masters swim team will meet a few times a week and generally has a coach shared among the swimmers. You can get feedback about your swimming from the other members, and you can get great advice about how to improve. This is a cheaper option that will help you gain some important knowledge.

If a coach is just not in the cards, become very familiar with YouTube and other online resources. Look up swim drills and exercises you can do in the water to develop a natural stroke and kick. Get some video of yourself in the pool and compare some of your techniques to the lessons in YouTube videos. You can learn a lot by seeing what you are doing and then learning drills to fix any issues.

The thing to remember with swimming is that no level of fitness can overcome a bad swim stroke. Conversely, a great stroke can make you faster without many fitness requirements.

How do you find a coach or a team? Start with Google and social media groups. Go to as many free triathlon-related functions as you can find. You will meet people who can help you along the way. Introduce yourself, and let people know you are looking to become more involved in the tri community. Triathletes like to talk about their training, so you will probably have recommendations from coaches or teams within a few minutes.

Before settling on a coach, it's helpful to know a little bit about your training preferences and abilities. It's good to have a general idea of your pace for running to start, as well as being aware of your skills on a bike and in the pool.

Finding a coach is like dating. You don't want to commit to anyone until you've learned about them first. Never commit to a coach before understanding their training style. Ask about attending a group function first or only paying for a week's trial before signing a contract for coaching. Some coaches are very intense. Other coaches are laid-back and chill. Coaches come in every variety, just like athletes, and it is important to learn about each coach you are considering.

Remember that coaches do not need to be local in order to be helpful. Sometimes, the best thing a coach can do for you is just ask you how your workout was and get you talking about your workouts, then give you feedback in a way that is constructive. Your coach does not need to be present to do that.

If you do choose to hire a coach or work with a team coach, be willing to talk to them. Communication is the only way to have a coach/client relationship that works. Don't be afraid to hurt their feelings if you did not complete a workout as planned. Rather, be honest about what went wrong and where your mind was. Your coach will need to know in order to adapt your training.

CHAPTER 7:

NUTRITION

Possibly the most controversial topic regarding triathlon training is nutrition. It's difficult to write a chapter and try to encompass all of the various thoughts about what to eat as a triathlete, so I will try to cover the basics and give you the best advice I can regarding nutrition: **learn as you go and do what works for you.**

There are a few rules of nutrition for endurance sports. You are going to need to provide your body with fuel. Your body is strangely good at adapting to fuel sources, but you don't want to switch sources the day before a race. Once you have established some eating routines, it's all right to try different things, but try not to make any big changes less than a week or so before a race.

There are two main fuel sources for our bodies: carbohydrates and fats. Carbohydrates are things like sugars and starches from rice, grains, fruits, and treats. These are your body's default fuel source because they are easy to break down and can be converted into energy quickly. They are also used up quickly, so during a race it's important to have a source of carbohydrates approximately once per hour in order to keep your body going.

Some athletes will take carbs to an extreme and do something called "carb-loading" the night before a race. This is generally eating concentrated carbohydrate energy as a way to give your body as much usable energy as possible for the race. On most training days, you are not going to want to eat full plates of carbohydrates. Generally, eat the bulk of your carb foods right around your workouts — before or after—and then eat more proteins and fats during the rest of the day.

Fueling your body with carbohydrates will give you fast, easy energy that you can put towards big efforts, but your fuel will burn up fast. Great sources of carbohydrates include:

- ✔ rice
- ✔ sweet potatoes
- ✔ fruit
- ✔ vegetables
- ✔ energy gels/chews

The other option for fuel in your body is fat. It takes anywhere from three days to two weeks for your body to go into ketosis, which is the state when your body will start using fat as a fuel source rather than looking for carbohydrates first. Forcing your body to use fat as fuel is often referred to as a keto diet. It requires eliminating carbohydrates from your diet for days at a time. There are some benefits to this. It is great for weight loss. Additionally, because fat is a slow-burning energy source, you won't have to eat as often to maintain your level of activity. One thing to consider, though, is that fat will not allow your body to access fast bursts of power or speed. This means that you can train for longer periods, but you will not be able to go as hard at any given time. Your body just won't have the energy.

Great sources of fat as fuel include:

- oils
- nut butters
- meats
- avocados

As I mentioned before, if you choose to alter your diet significantly, do it early and not the week before a race.

What about eating day to day? Again, there are so many various and differing ideas that I would never be able to cover everything. A general rule of thumb is to eat when you are hungry, and eat real food that does not come from a box or a can.

As an athlete, it is often easier to look at food in reference to how it makes you feel during your workouts. I recommend keeping a log of some general things you have eaten around the time you train to get a better understanding of what works and does not work for you and your stomach. Trust me, you do not want to need to rush to a bathroom during a run. You also do not want to throw up peanut butter during a bike ride or experience stomach cramps during a swim. As you experiment with foods, remember what helps your training and what hurts your body.

A few things to note about foods — nothing is off-limits as long as you can moderate yourself. If you are eating something every day, that is not a treat, it is part of your diet. It's okay to have desserts and sweets as a treat, but don't make it an everyday thing.

When you track your food, there are some factors you want to consider. First, when did you eat it during the day, and when did you eat it in relation to your workout? What workout was it — a swim, bike, run, or other? How much did you eat? Was this a full meal or a small snack? How did you feel after eating? How did you feel about an hour after eating? How did you feel during your workout?

These are important things to note because something like eating a steak in the evening after training might be a great way to help you feel full and ready for bed, or it might make you feel heavy and sluggish. Keep track of these things so that you can make an informed choice later, knowing how this meal or snack will make you feel. Knowledge is power in this case.

Does eating nuts before a workout make your stomach cramp, or are nuts a good fuel source for you? Does eating too much fruit before a run make you need to stop and find a bathroom a mile in? Does too much liquid in your stomach make you feel nauseated during a swim? All these things should be considered when planning out your meals and snacks for a day.

Once you know how various foods affect your body and your training, focus on eating quality foods that provide you with energy and do not make you feel sick during your workouts. Then eat other foods during the times of day when you don't need to worry about training, such as foods that might feel heavier or be harder to digest, like salads or meats.

For more information about proper nutrition for triathlon training, I suggest finding some food guides online. There are tons of free recipes and cookbooks. Test some out, and find something that works for you. You are just starting out, and it is silly to think you will eat the same diet as a professional athlete, so forgive yourself if you don't have a perfect meal plan. At this stage, you are still learning about your body and what will work for you.

After your first few triathlons, if you choose to become more serious about the sport or investigate longer distances, take time to look into more specific meal plans. Once you have a better understanding about how your body responds to different foods, you can invest in more specialized nutrition plans. Women's bodies are so diverse and so different, so it is silly to assume that one meal plan would work for everyone. Just follow the general rules:

- ✔ Food is your fuel.
- ✔ Eat when you are hungry; stop eating before you are overly full.
- ✔ Eat real foods that come from the ground or animals, rather than a factory.
- ✔ Keep treats a treat — not a daily thing.

CHAPTER 8:

PREPARING FOR THE RACE

As a beginner triathlete, the biggest moment of your training is when it all comes together and you head out on your first race. However, before you can get to that point, you'll need to be aware of a few things that make racing a triathlon different from training each discipline individually. THe following are a few things you'll want to consider incorporating into your training to prepare you mentally and physical for your first triathlon.

BRICK WORKOUTS

From the first day of training, you are working on three disciplines individually. You are going to do a swim workout, a run workout, or a bike workout. You'll need to improve your abilities in all three of these sports to complete your first tri. In addition, you will need to learn how to transition from swimming to riding, and riding to running.

A workout that consists of two or more triathlon disciplines at a time is called a "brick workout." Generally, the time spent in each sport is shorter, and the focus of a brick workout is to learn how it feels to adapt to a new style of athleticism after you are already tired. Traditionally, a brick workout is broken into twenty-minute segments for each sport.

Swim for twenty minutes then hop out of the pool and hop on a bike as fast as you are able. Granted, this isn't always easy if you swim in a gym, so a stationary bike will do. Another option to get a feel for moving around on your feet right out of the water is to walk around the pool after each lap towards the end of your swim workout. This can give you the same sensation you will have in the first transition during your race (the swim-to-bike transition, often referred to as T1) . Getting out of the water can sometimes be a little disorienting and make you feel a little dizzy. It is important to become familiar with this feeling before the day of your race.

Bike/run bricks are easier to implement. You can do two types of bricks for this transition. Ride for twenty minutes, then run for twenty minutes, and repeat; or break your workout into just two segments and bike until you are exhausted, then start into your run. The benefit of doing a full bike workout is that it trains your mind how to respond to running once you get off the bike with tired legs. The run does not need to be hard for this type of brick. You are focusing more on learning the feeling of running right after riding.

TRANSITION WORKOUTS

Even more important than brick workouts is practicing your actual transitions. During this time, it is not so important to have long workouts, but rather to become familiar with the wardrobe changes required for each transition. This is especially important because you don't want to forget something important like your helmet or race number. You also don't want to be a burden to the person next to you at the bike racks, so practicing each transition helps you become a more considerate racer.

TRANSITION 1 (T1)

T1 is your transition from swimming to riding. In your transition area, you will have your bike hanging on a bike rack. Hang your bike up by the front nose of the saddle. You will have an area under your bike with your cycling shoes. Your helmet will be somewhere that makes it impossible to forget (hanging on your handlebars or covering your shoes). Do not forget your helmet. Many races will disqualify you if you sit on your bike without your helmet. If you want socks, gloves, or sunglasses, place them somewhere easily accessible.

You will run/walk from the swim area to the transition area wearing your tri kit or race suit, a swim cap, and goggles. You may also have flip-flops or slip-on shoes if they are allowed in the race. You may also be wearing a wetsuit.

Unzip your wetsuit, and strip that down by pulling it inside out, over your body to your waist as you enter transition. When you reach your bike, you can pull your wetsuit off over your legs. Most people take their wetsuit off in a hurry by stepping on it with one foot and pulling the other foot out a bit, then alternating step/pulls back and forth until it is off. You should have your clothes for the remainder of the race on under your wetsuit. If you are not wearing a wetsuit for the race, then this will be a much faster transition. Remove your goggles and cap at the same time and *put on your helmet*. Do not forget your helmet. At this time, put on your footwear, gloves, sunglasses, or any other needed accessories. Sometimes you might not want to wear socks while riding because they can be difficult to put on with wet feet. Generally, a good option is to put talcum powder into your shoes to prevent blisters. Your race number will be on your bike so there is no need to worry about that yet.

Pull your bike off the rack without damaging your wetsuit or running shoes. You'll walk/run your bike until you've reached the designated mounting zone, which will be marked outside of transition. You should never be riding your bike in transition. Once again, do not forget your helmet and make sure it is buckled.

You can prepare for this transition by practicing taking off your wetsuit and swim stuff, putting on your helmet and riding gear, and then walking your bike one-hundred yards before mounting. Take a little spin, then come back and practice your next transition.

TRANSITION 2 (T2)

The switch between riding and running is generally faster than T1. There will be a designated dismount zone. You must dismount your bike in this zone to ensure everyone is safe in transition. Once you are off your bike, you can start unbuckling your helmet. Do not remove your helmet before dismounting. Hang your bike on the bike rack in the same place you retrieved it from in T1. If T1 and T2 are in different places, the racks are often numbered; find where you have your run gear set up and rack your bike there.

Once your bike is hanging on the rack, you can change into running shoes and put on your race belt with your race number. If you did not put socks on with your cycling shoes, you can still put on socks now. Take off your helmet and any cycling accessories you do not need for the run, and head out. You'll place your helmet and cycling shoes underneath your racked bike.

Practice this transition a few times at a park or somewhere you can easily ride and run very short distances safely.

Put these two transitions together and practice both at the same time. You will learn how you like to set up your transition area, and you will develop a style for how you get changed. Do what works for you, and play around to make sure this part of the race is not a problem for you on race day.

WATCH A RACE

A great way to ease fears about your first tri is to attend a race to see what it will be like. As a spectator, you have no responsibilities and you can enjoy the day without stress. Additionally, it is especially helpful to view a race from the other side. Watch how the athletes set up transitions and how they warm up before the race starts.

If you know someone in a race, head out with them for the whole process of race prep and help them get their wetsuit and race numbers on. You can learn a lot by helping someone get ready. Talk to them about timing and when they warm up for each sport, what they do to check their bike before they put it in the rack, and how far in advance they get into the water.

You can get ideas about how to set up your transition areas by looking at the areas of the other athletes. Get ideas you can try later to get a feel for your own preferred methods.

Another great way to view an event before your own race is by volunteering. Race directors love volunteers and are always eager for people to help set up bike racks, mark the course, lay out cones the day before, help athletes write race numbers on their arms, and hand out water at aid stations on race day. There are a ton of volunteer opportunities that give you a different perspective on what it means to be a triathlete. Volunteers are what make events fun because they are often the only people on the racecourse. It's so helpful to have happy, excited volunteers who cheer and provide upbeat energy. You'll see how much fun the volunteers can bring to a race.

However you choose to watch a race, the goal is to build knowledge because this will alleviate fear and anxiety. Going into your first race will tie your stomach in knots, but the more experience you have understanding all sides of the event, the more prepared you will feel.

FIND A SUPPORT CREW

Triathletes need help sometimes. If you are training with a team, you might have a lot of people at the event who can support you. It's always helpful to plan ahead and ask some friends and family to come be your crew. This is more than just moral support. These people can help you make sure you have everything ready before you race, such as extra tube and tire levels in case you get a flat, or make sure your water is filled and your food is in your pockets. They can find where the results are posted and help get you snacks after the race too.

Before you start, your brain might go a little fuzzy, and you might not be able to think clearly. Ask your crew to make sure you're warming up and that you are ready to go when the whistle blows. Give them a briefing ahead of time on what they will need to know on race day. This crew is going to be able to think more clearly and will be able to help you with all the little details that might slip your mind race morning. Make sure this support crew reads Chapter 9: Race Morning Prep.

After the race, you are going to be tired and it is incredibly helpful to have a supportive crew to help you collect your wits and belongings to ensure you don't forget anything at the race venue.

The support crew can also hold things for you while you are racing, such as a wallet or a jacket. Depending on the weather and the venue, you'll want to make sure everything is safe with someone you trust.

Use your support crew for anything else you can think of during the race. Let them know that you need them to be your eyes, ears, and brain for parts of the day. There are plenty of times where it is the support crew that makes a first race a success.

KNOW THE COURSE

Again, knowledge, alleviates fears. Learn the course for your race before the day of the race. Most courses are posted online, and you can either drive around the course or you can ride it. It's not necessary to have the course memorized, but it's recommended to have an idea of where it goes. It can be very scary to be unsure of the next turn, and there is not always going to be someone in front of you or with you who can help. Most racecourses are marked very well, and you should be able to see arrows or cones to indicate where to ride or run. Every opportunity to be prepared is helpful though, so look at a race map and know the route before race day.

It's not always possible to get into the water to swim the exact course before race day because buoys are not often set out until the night before the race. Still, be aware of what is expected for the swim. Sometimes a swim is one or two laps. You'll need to know if you are swimming clockwise or counterclockwise and where the swim start and exit are located. Lastly, you'll want to know beforehand what type of start is used. Will you have time to acclimate to the water, or do swimmers jump in or run in from the beach?

FOOD AND DRINKS

I spoke about this briefly before, but it is important to know what you can and cannot eat during a race. The worst time to find out you cannot eat something is in the middle of the course.

There are many different endurance-sport energy bars, chews, drinks, protein bars, or gels. How will you know what you'd like to use to refuel yourself during your race? You want to know going into a race that whatever you are putting into your body during the race isn't going to give you trouble. It's much harder to find an emergency pit stop during the race than during training. You want to know this before a race because everyone handles food differently.

You will need two major things in your body during a race. First, you will need a source of energy. If you are choosing to eat carbohydrates as your energy source, make sure you have something to munch on during the bike ride. Test out gels or chews. These tend to be packaged in containers that make them easy to eat during a bike ride. When shopping for some energy chews or gels, get two that look interesting to you. If you like something and it makes you feel good, you will have another one ready for you on race day. This means you won't have to worry about shopping or food prep right before your race.

You will also need to ensure that you have plenty of electrolytes to replace the salts you lose in sweat. Sports drinks are a great way to replace these electrolytes, but there are a few things to consider. Often sports drinks pack in a lot of extra sugar, which you might not want during your race. The same rule applies with sports drinks as with calorie sources. Try a few things during training to make sure you like the taste and the way it makes you feel because you do *not* want to find out that you cannot tolerate a drink in the middle of your race. Many drinks come in small single-serving pouches or in large containers with a scoop to mix with water. I recommend finding a drink you like by trying various single-serving pouches, then consider purchasing the bulk container.

Consider the taste of the sports products during a workout. Some things taste great when you are in the middle of a workout but terrible to just drink during the day. Also, consider how it settles in your stomach. Lastly, consider how many calories you need. Generally, you will want to consume about one hundred calories of carbohydrates for every hour you are working out. If you are choosing to use a keto diet you won't need to eat much during the ride, but you will still need to replenish your electrolytes.

Plan what you can eat before your race as well. If you want to eat breakfast before racing, play around during training with foods that digest easily, like toast. You'll need to have a protein source as well, so experiment to see what you can eat and how long you will need to wait before you can hop in the water after eating.

JUST KEEP SWIMMING

For your first triathlon, it is extra important to be hyper-aware of what to expect for the swim, and prepare accordingly. Most beginner triathletes say that the worst part of the race is the swim. The swim causes panic attacks more than any other part of the race. What is so intimidating about the swim? It's easy to think that if you have been swimming for months and you feel comfortable in a pool, you will naturally be able to jump into open water and be fine. Swimming is swimming, right? Wrong.

Open-water swimming can be very intimidating if you have never done it before and if the water is especially cold. Often, plunging your face into very cold water triggers something similar to a panic attack for many people. This is pretty normal,

especially for beginners, and it can be worked through with proper training. This is why it is important to practice open-water swimming whenever you get the chance. To ease the initial shock of putting your face into the cold water, it helps to breathe out slowly and expel all the air from your lungs, then come back out and take a great big breath. If you can do this right before the start of the race, it may help to quell some fears. Some races let you wade into the water before the swim starts, which gives you time to submerge your face and blow some bubbles to let your heart and lungs grow accustomed to the shock.

Even if you do not start the race in the water and you have to run in from the beach or dive in from a dock, it is still better to take a few moments at the start of the swim to breathe out and regroup. Regain control over your heartbeat and breathing. This lessens that feeling of panic.

Stay towards the back of the swim wave if you have to. As a beginner, you don't need to fight off elbows and feet trying to race towards the front of the group. There is a lot of chaos in the water and that can add to the panicky feeling, so just take it easy at the back. If you are a strong swimmer, work your way up by passing people.

You might be swimming with a wetsuit for your race. Depending on the type of wetsuit you are wearing, it could impact your stroke and your kick. Wetsuits are extra buoyant, but they are harder to move in so it will be harder to move your shoulders and arms for a stroke. Get a few good swims in with a wetsuit, if you can, to learn how your stroke will change and notice how much of a difference it makes.

In open water you are not going to have a pool lane to follow. In fact, you might not be able to see anything at all in the water if it is murky. You might see fish or other weed-type plants in the water beneath you. You might even touch a fish, although if you stay towards the back of the group that's unlikely since the fish will hide from the commotion that just passed. A few things to note about why it is a little unnerving to lose the sense of vision in the water: you might not be able to see the bottom, and you might be swimming in the wrong direction. When you can't see the bottom of the body of water, it's tempting to lose confidence and feel a little unsafe. Train in open water to become comfortable with the feeling of being in a large open space without having a wall or the bottom of the pool for support. Practice just treading water and getting your breathing under control *before* you jump into the water for your race.

What about swimming in the wrong direction? Trust me, it happens. Professional athletes all have a story to share about when they felt great in the water, only to realize they were not even close to the actual swim route. Open-water swimming is a great time to practice sighting—picking your head up and looking forward for a brief moment rather than breathing to the side. This is sometimes really difficult in races because generally the swim is early in the morning, and the sun is still right above the horizon. Sometimes sighting means you are looking directly into the sun and trying to find a buoy in all that blindness. All the more reason to practice swimming in open waters to become a bit more at ease with estimating where you are in the water.

The main take away about swimming is that it can be the cause for you to want to quit before the race even gets started. Don't let this be the case. Fight the fear by having knowledge of what it will be like in the open water. Practice getting out and swimming in similar conditions to what you will be swimming on race day.

CHAPTER 9:

RACE MORNING PREP

Good morning, you've made it to race day. This is the day you've been preparing for since you had the wild idea that you wanted to do a triathlon. Today is the day that you will climb your personal mountain, and you will overcome the struggle and see the top of the world. Today, the sun will shine brighter than it has ever shone (even if the sun isn't shining). At the end of today, you have the right to call yourself a badass. You are accomplishing something great, and you have been preparing for this day with your sweat, blood, and tears. This is it.

The first thing you'll notice is that you absolutely don't want to eat because your stomach is in knots, and you can't imagine getting any food in. That's a terrible feeling. I know, I've been there. You feel like you can't even swallow because your mouth is dry and your throat is working overtime to keep down the vomit that is trying to escape.

Fight that feeling. The first thing you are going to need to remember on race morning is that you need to have enough food inside your body to give you the energy you will need during your race. You might need coffee or eggs or bacon. Whatever you've chosen as your pre-race meal, eat as much of that as you can. Take small bites and swallow carefully. Resist the bile that is threatening to come up. Once you start swimming and get into your rhythm, this feeling will instantly disappear and your body will go into a completely different mode. You'll be in race mode. You'll be pumped full of adrenaline and excitement, and all of this nausea will feel like the distant past. This is only temporary.

I know that's easy to say, but it is true. Try some visualization exercises to help calm your nerves. You've done the prep work, and you've attended some races. Close your eyes and visualize things that can go wrong. Yes, picture the problems you might encounter. Then picture what you will do to get past those challenges. Picture the successes after you complete your first triathlon. Imagine yourself overcoming every obstacle, and really let your body feel what it will be like to push past any pain you might feel.

Some athletes choose to do visualization exercises while wearing headphones or something to block out noise. If this is available to you, do that. Find a quiet place and picture how sweet it will taste to run across that finish line with your friends and loved ones cheering your name. Feel the weight of that finisher medal as it touches your chest for the first time. Visualize the pain that is the only thing in your way, and picture yourself pushing through the pain and pressing onward no matter what.

Your mind might be in a little bit of a fog this morning, or you might be hyper-aware of every detail. No matter the state of your mind, there are a few things on race day to think about, besides the vomity feeling.

COMMUNICATE WITH YOUR FANS

Your friends and family will want to be able to watch you at specific parts of the day, but you might also need them to be available for you before or after the race. Make sure everyone is aware of where they should be and when. Sometimes it is easiest for spectators to stay near the transition area, but if your fans are choosing to be on the course to watch you race, just make sure they know where to find you afterwards. This is especially true if you are depending on someone for a ride. You won't have a phone with you, so communicate now about plans for after the race.

WARM-UP

Most of your warm-up can be dedicated to the swim. Take your bike out for a quick spin, though, to make sure the tires are filled to the correct pressure for the road or trail conditions. Check your brakes and make sure all axles are secured and quick release levers are not loose. Remember to always wear your helmet, even for the warm-up. The last thing to do on your bike warm-up is to change gears until you are in the gear you want to start riding in. It is no fun to jump on a bike to charge off up a steep climb only to realize you are in the hardest gear.

For a quick reference of things to check on your bike:

- ✔ tire pressure
- ✔ spare tube and tire levers, if needed
- ✔ quick release levers
- ✔ brakes
- ✔ appropriate starting gear
- ✔ chain lube
- ✔ handlebar caps: These are the little end caps that seal off the ends of your handlebars. It is required that these be covered to prevent serious damage in an accident. Quarters fit nicely on the end of handlebars if you do not have these caps.
- ✔ water bottles filled appropriately (sports drink, water, or both).
- ✔ nutrition available: Some gels or chews can be taped to the bike with electrical tape or stored in a pouch on the bike. You can also leave your nutrition handy for you to grab in transition.

Next, do a quick jog around. You could do this before riding as well, but you want to get your legs warmed up and moving.

Your swim warm-up will be after you are done setting up your transition and everything is ready for your race.

SETTING UP TRANSITION

By now you should have practiced a few mock transitions in your training, so you should have a pretty clear idea of how to lay out your gear to make it available for you during each discipline of the race. Each race is different. Sometimes you must hang your bike on the rack assigned to your race number. Other times, the racks are first come, first served. Generally, bike racks have six to seven bikes per rack, but again, this is different for every race. If you have questions, there are almost always volunteers in the transition area, or you can ask a fellow athlete.

Things to remember in your transition area:

- ✔ riding shoes
- ✔ socks, if wanted
- ✔ bike hanging on bike rack by the nose of the saddle — bikes are generally arranged staggered so every other bike points in the opposite direction.
- ✔ HELMET
- ✔ gloves, if needed
- ✔ food/drink (probably already attached to your bike)
- ✔ running shoes
- ✔ race number belt with number attached
- ✔ hat and sunglasses, if needed
- ✔ towel: Many athletes like to lay everything out on a small towel to help define their space and to wipe their feet off before putting on cycling shoes.

Before leaving transition for the final time, check the air in the tires of your bike, make sure everything is lined up and easy to access, and double-check that your bike is in the right starting gear. In transition, you will need to get your race number written on your arm or swim cap (depending on how the race director planned it). There are generally volunteers helping with that.

There is one final thing you need to do before you leave transition. You need to know where your transition area is in relation to where you will enter (from either the swim or the bike). Stand at the swim entrance opening of the transition area, and use any visual reference you can to find your way back to your transition area. This might be counting the racks (three racks to the right, the second rack in on the left), or it might be distinguishing features (right after the toilets at the end of the row on the right). Do not try to find your transition area in relation to the other bikes around it because some of the bikes will be gone when you enter transition. Everything inside will be different, and you do not want to wander up and down aisles in T1 or T2 trying to find your things. Repeat this process for the bike entrance.

GEAR UP TO SWIM

If you are wearing a wetsuit, now is the time to suit up. Wetsuits may look pretty straightforward, but it is actually a bit tricky to squeeze into one. Start at the feet and carefully (without using fingernails, which can puncture the material) pull the wetsuit legs up over your calves as high as you need to get it. Continue to make tiny pulls until you can get the wetsuit over the rest of your legs and torso. Sometimes spraying your body with cooking spray helps slide a wetsuit into place. A wetsuit should fit tight to your skin, especially in the crotch and shoulder areas. You should be able to raise your arm up without extra material pulling it down in the armpit. Likewise, you should be able to kick without feeling hindered by too much wetsuit between your legs.

Wetsuits sometimes rub on your neck when you breathe in the water so some athletes will put Vaseline around the edges of the wetsuit to prevent chafing and rubbing.

Next, style your hair in a way that will fit under your swim cap and then your bike helmet. For short hair, sometimes it's best to just tie it back into a low ponytail or leave your hair down. If you have long hair, an easy hairstyle is to wear a single braid down your back, or two braids on either side that are low enough that they won't hinder your helmet. To help keep your hair nice, rub a little leave-in conditioner in your hair before pulling it back.

If you have a choice, choose goggles that are appropriate for the sunlight. You might want to swim with tinted goggles to see a bit better, or if you are swimming in low light, you can invest in goggles that have a slight yellow tint to make the world a little brighter.

Once you get in the water, remember that the panicky feeling you get from the temperature and the pressure of the wetsuit is a natural reflex of your body. It is not an actual panic attack, but it could be if you don't relax and breathe through it. Once submerged in the water, blow bubbles and breathe all the air out of your lungs. Then, come up for air and take a huge breath. Continue this until your heartbeat becomes more regular and the tightness of your chest loosens. Feel free to do this even during a race. Remember, you are here with a goal to complete this triathlon. If you need to stop for a moment to regain control, that's okay. It is perfectly acceptable to take a second to breathe and calm your body. Open-water swimming is new and scary, and you are not the only one who feels this way. Everyone has experienced it at some point in their triathlon career.

Warm up in the water as close to the start time as you are allowed before everyone is cleared out to prepare for the start of the race.

AND THEY'RE OFF

Once that first gun goes off, it's tempting to bolt out of the watery gate and swim ahead as fast as possible. Take it easy. Find your pace or breathe and blow bubbles if you need to for a second. You can always increase your speed as you go, but for right now, just find the pace that is comfortable for you.

There are places you can stop and catch your breath. There is always a lot of water support during the swim phase to ensure the safety of the athletes. You can stop and hold onto the stand-up paddle boards or the boats along the way. Take your time. Do what feels right for your abilities. If you are feeling competitive, then try to swim in the group or ahead of people, but if you prefer to go slow and just focus on finishing, that's great too.

Don't forget to sight as you swim. You can't always trust that the person in front of you is sighting. Don't follow someone only to let them lead you in the wrong direction. Look ahead, and frequently assess which direction you need to go. In some bodies of water, you might need to sight a lot because of currents and waves, while in others you might be okay to sight just occasionally. Regardless, don't forget to sight your swim.

After you exit the swim, you might feel a little dizzy. Head towards T1 and mentally try to go over exactly how you will go through transition. Don't give even a tiny thought to the run yet. You need to focus on the bike phase. Stay focused on what you are doing at every step. It's natural to get ahead of yourself, but it's important to stay consistent and keep your mind in the present.

T1 is a good time to eat or drink. This transition will take a little more time, which means that the food has time to settle without being jostled around while you race. Get some calories to make sure you have enough energy.

You've practiced your transition before the race, so you know how to take your wetsuit off by standing on the opposite leg and pulling your foot out a little at a time, then switching legs. You know to put your helmet on first to make sure you don't forget it. Then, get your shoes on and any other accessories you want or need, like gloves or sunglasses. For longer triathlons, someone may be available to apply sunscreen, but for shorter tris, you can do this yourself if you need it at all.

Onto the bike. At first, you might feel a little weak because the blood needed to bring energy to your legs was sending all your energy to your arms during the swim. Your body needs to adjust and start redirecting this power to your lower half. Once your legs find a good rhythm, you'll be able to really focus on riding and forget the swim.

Don't dwell on how you did in the swim. Pay attention to the bike right now. Eat and drink when you can . This is an especially great time to hydrate because it is generally easier to drink while riding than it is while running.

After your ride, you will dismount in the dismount zone. Never ride your bike in transition for the safety of the other athletes on foot. Rack your bike in the same place you got it, right over your transition gear. Change your shoes, and remove your helmet. Strap on your race number belt then head out onto your fun (I mean run).

Your legs will feel like Jello, and you will have a funny running gait at first while your legs adjust from the bike to the ground. It is almost like your legs still want to pedal, but they are running at the same time, so your knees just move extra high, and your cadence might feel a little off. Again, this is normal, and this funny feeling goes away quickly as your body realizes what you are doing and adapts.

This is your last discipline. At the end of your run, you get to cross the finish line and join the ranks of triathletes. If you have any proverbial matches left in your legs, burn them at the end of this run. Use the fuel you have remaining to reach that finish line. You can collapse in pain on the other side, but you are not going to let yourself stop until you've gotten there.

MENTAL RESETS

If at any point you feel like this is too much and you want to quit, it is probably just minor panic from your brain. Your brain is trained to avoid anything difficult that might hurt you. As far as your brain knows, you are hurting. You brain will try to convince you to stop.

My best advice: stop. But only stop for a short moment. If you are swimming, tread water and catch your breath. If you are riding, ease up on the power and coast or even put a foot down and all-out stop. During your run, there is no shame in walking for a bit. What you are doing is telling your brain, "Yes, this hurts, but I am not hurting myself. See? I'm all right. As soon as I stop, I'm safe again and I'm not in danger." Your brain will thank you and will regain that excitement to keep going and finish this thing you've started. The image of yourself reaching the end is a powerful tool for helping your mind get back to the race.

As you get better at training, you can train yourself to go through this little brain reset/reminder without needing to stop. Right now, though, don't be afraid to do whatever you have to in order to fully finish the race.

CHAPTER 10:

YOU'VE FINISHED. NOW WHAT

You've finished your first triathlon. What a great accomplishment. You are on top of the world and you can do anything ... until tomorrow.

There is a natural cycle of emotions surrounding your triathlon. Before the race, you will probably be excited and nervous. Moments after the event, you will be thrilled and hyper, full of adrenaline and excitement. The following day, as that adrenaline wears off, your body will feel like you've hit a wall. You might be sore on an entirely new level, and you will feel completely exhausted. That's perfectly normal.

Plan a day to relax and recoup. An event like a triathlon is a big ordeal, and your body pays the price. Let it recover. Enjoy some good food, and take some naps if you need to.

You might also be feeling a little down emotionally. That's also normal. If you are prone to depression, try to combat this feeling with friends or light activities that help you stay at peace, but also allow yourself to feel a little sluggish and low. This is a post-race side effect and it does not last very long. Your brain needs to repair just as much as your body does. Watch some funny movies and avoid stress. You are recovering mentally as well as physically, and your mind has had a lot of stress lately.

That after-race sadness is something that many athletes are aware of. Professionals plan days after a race to go over their race results, but as a novice, try writing down all the great things that happened during the race. For a few days, try to really let your mind dwell on the amazing parts of the day. A few days later, if you choose, you can go back and analyze things that you could do better or things that did not go well.

This is the perfect time to learn about ways to improve. This is also the time for you to consider doing another race. Has the tri bug bit you, or are you content to be done after one race?

If you do choose to do another race, start looking for races now, while you are excited about the next steps. You might feel a little lost, as if you don't know what to do now that you no longer have a specific goal to work towards. That is when finding another race or another event will come in handy. Consider how you felt about the race you just completed, and decide if that is a feeling you want to experience over again.

Most of all, remember that after a race your emotions will be all over the place. This may be a sensation you understand from other experiences in your life, or it may be completely new. If you are feeling like an emotional wreck, find a group of other women to talk to about your experience. Other triathletes understand the mood you're in, and they can help you by talking things through. There are tons of triathlon groups on Facebook to join, or talk to your own support group. You are feeling things that are completely normal. It can be a little shocking to go from full adrenaline euphoria after a race to emotionally wiped out within the span of twenty-four hours.

CHAPTER 11:

WHAT ABOUT INJURIES

Every athlete is afraid of being hurt badly enough that they can no longer train. That is a fear that is common in beginners, experienced athletes, and pros. What happens when that silent fear becomes a reality?

It's safe to assume that at some point, you will have an ache or a pain that doesn't feel right. There is a difference between good pain and bad pain. The good pain is a welcome feeling because that is what makes us realize we are working hard and getting stronger. It is bad pain that makes our hearts stop and our stomachs jump into our chests. It's the bad pain that always comes with the question, "What if ... ?"

The first and most important thing is, *do not push through bad pain.* No single workout is worth the risk of seriously injuring yourself. For example, if your foot or ankle or knee hurts during a run, walk. The calories you are burning in continuing to push yourself are not enough to compensate for what you might have to miss if you injure yourself further.

Granted, this is very difficult to do, and I have heard countless stories of athletes who run on injuries which then result in stress fractures or worse. Take this as a warning that you will try to convince yourself that you are fine, but it is better to just take it easy for that workout and reassess when you are done.

The best way to combat injury is with knowledge. If something hurts, get it diagnosed. There are injuries that can actually be prevented by changing shoes or gait or having a proper bike fit, but you won't know this until you have the injury diagnosed by a professional. Don't just assume it will go away if you keep running or riding on it. Chances are it won't.

Once you know what the problem is, there are often things you can do to prevent irritating the injury, assuming you caught it early on. Take care of bad pain before it becomes something serious.

Rest, Ice, Compression, and Elevation (RICE) are your friends.

Rest — If something is bothering you, take a break. Luckily, as a triathlete, you have a couple other sports to train if one discipline makes the pain worse. Running is the general culprit for pains due to the stress on your joints. Take a few days off from your run training, and get some extra time on the bike or in the pool.

Ice — Prevent swelling of the affected area with some ice packs directly after a workout. Remember that after you have iced your joints, they will feel stiff, so don't move too quickly with cold joints. You can also alleviate swelling with ibuprofen, but use this with caution, as pain relievers can mask a more serious injury that should be taken care of.

Compression —ACE bandage wraps and sports wraps work great to keep your joints stabilized. You might also consider wearing compression clothing if your joints are prone to swelling. KT tape or other varieties of sports tape can add stability to your joints as well, and there are tons of videos to help you use these products properly.

Elevation — Raise the affected body part above your heart for a while to help keep the blood circulating. This is especially helpful for legs.

If you have been experiencing pain for a while, or you have been diagnosed with a serious injury, you might need to take some time off from training altogether. Training for a tri can increase pain from a completely unrelated injury, such as from a car accident. Whatever the injury is, always remember that your body needs your help to recover. Do not push harder than you need to. You have plenty of time to get back into training, but if your body needs to recover, you must allow it the time it needs. Your body has limited resources devoted to healing. Don't force your body to deal with healing you from a hard workout when it should be dedicating all its healing powers to your injury.

During your downtime, you will have some great opportunities that you normally would not have. You have the time to read and learn about your sports. You can look up recipes and training plans. You can offer advice and support to others. Use this time to learn about other aspects of the sport that can help you once you are back into training. If you have a very specific injury, take this time to learn all you can about that injury so you can provide what your body needs, plus some.

If your worst nightmare comes true and you are told that you will probably not race again, it's okay to grieve for the loss of your sport. Just like losing a loved one, giving up training for a triathlon is a huge loss. It is alright to be sad, but don't remain sad forever.

Your identity is not in what you do but in how you live your life. Triathlon might be a huge part of who you are, but it is not the only thing that defines you. Plus, you can still be very involved with the sport without competing by volunteering and offering support to other triathletes. There is always a loss of self whenever the ability to do something you love is taken away. You can refocus the energy, strength, and determination you used to train for a triathlon to build a new identity.

There are also huge technological leaps that allow injuries and disabilities to be overcome. Blind athletes are setting world records. Paralyzed athletes are climbing mountains. There are people who love the challenge of helping athletes get into a sport they love despite barriers. You might have to become comfortable with a different way of training, but there is not much in the world these days that will cut you off from triathlon completely.

CHAPTER 12:

WISDOM AND ADVICE

As someone who was very recently a beginner triathlete, I want to leave you with some pieces of wisdom and advice to make this experience the best of your life.

HAVE FUN

I am very familiar with the urge to compare yourself to others. As women, we do it all the time, but it's not always healthy. In this sport, it truly does not matter what you look like. There is no one laughing about your hairstyle or lack of fashion. You do not need to be prettier or taller or sexier than anyone else. What you need to do is let the wind fill your heart as you ride. You need to let the water tickle your skin until you laugh. Let the sound of your feet on the road become the sound of applause for what you have done.

Let go of comparisons and just have fun. Enjoy the pain of a great workout and the thrill of knowing you are getting stronger and faster. Smile, and be you without thought or care about how you look or comparing yourself to others.

SUFFERING MAKES YOU FEEL ALIVE

There are a lot of things in this world that cause us to go numb to the world around us. We just go about our routines. We go to work, maybe have some free time, eat, sleep, repeat. The suffering from training is a spark of real feeling in our lives. Hold onto that. Whenever it hurts and you want to stop, take hold of that struggle and embrace it because this is how you are going to truly live.

MAKE FRIENDS

The triathlon community is more like a family than a group of people competing in the same sport. These people understand you, and they want to see you succeed. This is where you can find a tribe that will ease the loneliness of life in the modern age.

Don't shy away from making friends at races or events. Find others in your position on social media and reach out to them. You never know where your best friend is waiting.

PASS IT ON

Triathlon easily becomes a passion. Don't hold that passion close; let it explode out of you and affect everyone you know.

If you have to, you could even write your own book for the next generation, because this sport is truly life changing.

Good luck! I'm so glad you had the idea to do a triathlon.

TRI ATH LON

Reviews and feedback help improve this book and the author. If you enjoy this book, we would greatly appreciate it if you could take a few moments to share your opinion and post a review on Amazon.

Printed in Great Britain
by Amazon